THE
HELPER'S NOTES:
Volume One

———

Author: D. Alt

Co-Author: Benjamin A.J.A.

Gotham Books

30 N Gould St.
Ste. 20820, Sheridan, WY 82801
https://gothambooksinc.com/

Phone: 1 (307) 464-7800

© 2024 *D. Alt*. All rights reserved.

No part of this book may be reproduced, stored in a retrieval system, or transmitted by any means without the written permission of the author.

Published by Gotham Books (July 12, 2024)

ISBN: 979-8-3302-8113-8 (P)
ISBN: 979-8-3302-8114-5 (E)

Because of the dynamic nature of the Internet, any web addresses or links contained in this book may have changed since publication and may no longer be valid.

The views expressed in this work are solely those of the author and do not necessarily reflect the views of the publisher, and the publisher hereby disclaims any responsibility for them.

FOREWORD
Written by: Benjamin A.J.A.

Love mine; admire His.
Soon you won't be or act in haste as life's fruits unfold.
Do not accept another person's pressure.
He is just, just as you want it to be.
Study, meeting attendance and prayer.
Do not be overly excited when you have a plan, or when you have money.
If you're too fast the crash will be harder, the faster you go the harder the crash.
Our survival depends on our obedience.
Do not be afraid to take on your own responsibilities.
Do not be afraid to save your money.
Change your friends to those who will help you focus on becoming a better you.

DEDICATION

This book has been written to help, to assist, to heal, to uplift, and to open the hearts and minds of my readers and is therefore dedicated to you the reader.

Also, to my beautiful little Angel:

Aaliyah Alt

You are loved and greatly appreciated.

PREFACE

I started writing this book somewhere around 2012 with the intention of baring my soul, expressing my heart, and sharing my mind for so to leave behind my legacy. It quickly became something of far greater potential as I filled page after page with inspirational quotes, motivational phrases, words of wisdom and loving notes. The original version of the book was hand written in part, and transferred to typed.

I truly believe in the content of this book and hope that as you, the reader read and interpret what you read in your very own way that you can apply what you will learn into your life somehow and that you grow from the experience of reading these pages.

It also is my hopes that you share what you have learned with your friends and family so as one we grow together. It is love & light I send you.

He who is wise, knows knowledge is everywhere.

INTRODUCTION

    I personally wouldn't label this a self-help book so to speak. This book is more to remind you what you are, to inspire you, and to guide you along your journey. It is not persuasive or manipulative in its way. It states simple basic fundamental truths to awaken the inner you and open the heart and mind. One who is receptive and open to incoming information is more apt to grow, and to live more prosperously than the opposite of that would be.

You, are Loved.

Focus yourself on being positive, healthy and happy.
Center yourself so to speak and find your balance.
Become whole as one being, including mind,
body and soul.

One smile can kill one thousand frowns.

As we travel our paths and or time lines important is to
hold the best from the past, live in the present,
and always and in all ways look forward to the future.
It is as so what we think we become, therefore important
is to become the future you wish to see.

Listen to your heart, yet do censor with rational thought.

Of all things negative, negative emotion is amongst the
worst. Negativity is not fought or countered with
negativity, conversion of such is success.

Rush not that which is yet to be understood,
allow time for so to see.
Patience is a key to progression and achievement.

Become one, live whole truth.

Pursue positivity, both inside and out.
Our inner desires to be or become, or to create or establish, form the very world in which we live.

Do be positive.

True is the evolution of mentality, physicality, and spirituality. Control your destiny and define your outcome. Choose the course you wish to take and bring yourself to the desired destination.

Never allow fear to be a factor.
You can and will if you try wholeheartedly.
Free the mind, steady the heartbeat, breathe, and be.
Know that the impossible is possible as such is a mere obstacle and finding the proper path is key.

One of the greatest gifts we are,
or have been given is ourselves.

Meditation is medicine for the mind. Take the time to unclutter the thoughts and find peace within one's self before pursuing physical or spiritual activity.

Surround yourself with positivity, live, breathe, be, and become happiness.

Allow not the spread of negativity, breathe not it to life.

Learn to manage your emotion,
misdirection of such can be harmful to self.

Learn to value and appreciate the difference in the individuality and character of others.
Again, one of the greatest gifts we can receive is ourselves.

Lighten up, it is the way.

Hold onto your happiness, let it not be stolen.

When humanities general awareness has heightened and many are awoken you will see and you will know and begin to understand that which was previously unknown or uncomprehensible.

The aligning of paths and time lines and the straightening of that which has been made crooked will bring you peace and place into harmony life and all that is. It will also accelerate your educational growth as a whole through the sharing of thoughts and ideas.

To truly love another one must first know and love one's self. After learning or finding your path through life you can then find a very special correlation in another.

Do develop positive mentalities. Pursue positive thinking actively as this is key to a successful life.

No one was sent to earth with what you have or hold, do share yourself with the world. Do be you as it is within our differences rests vast possibilities.

Knowledge is power, it is commonly said that knowing is half the battle.

You cannot lie to your own soul, or lie to life forever. Lies are around for a limited time only.

**How you feel about yourself is in some aspect or to some degree how the world will feel about you.
When you feel good, you have a positive energy around you or a positive vibe so to speak.**

You cannot witness all of life's beauty with your head down. Keep your head up.

Happiness is attractive, do be that.
You are beautiful just the way you are.

Train your brain and learn to force negativity to exit.
It is true the more positive you think, the more positive
the thought or train of thought becomes.

**Raise your children as if they were to be your parents.
Meaning, instill within them the morals and values you so
wish they instill in their young for so to be carried on
from generation to generation.**

Extract from life the hatred and negativity,
and invest in it the love and positivity.

**Combat negativity in all ways.
Counter it and or convert it whenever possible.**

Create yourself or mold your character in, with,
and of positivity. Find or create your positive prime.

**Practice the purification of self
and do so to the point of thought.**

Do be kind, warm hearted, and loving to all.
You can never fully know what someone may be going
through just to be or become them.

Love is powerful, powerful is love.

Life is an adventure. Let not the current state of such,
or what seems to be the speed or pace of things discourage
you. Take time to gather your thoughts, take time to
collect yourself as you are to you your greatest gift.

No one deserves to be lonely.

Keep your dreams alive.
Every dream has been given for a reason.

Develop and promote positive, happy, healthy lifestyles.

Isolation is not healthy. Surround yourself with people
who love you, and care about you and your well-being.

Smile through the bad days, and laugh on the good ones.

There are times failure will be our greatest teacher.
Best is to acknowledge such as stepping stones to success.

Do know that when you introduce a new idea into physical reality and people are involved, evolution of said idea is involved as well.

Do introduce positivity in all forms while reducing negativity at the same time. Practice good mathematics.

Simple truths are generally easily stated and understood.

Do find a positive way to convert negative emotion or energy.

**Practice healthy living,
consciously make healthy decisions.**

Never place in place a period
where you know a question mark may exist.

**Control your conclusion, consciously make the choice
or decision to be what you want to be.
Pursue that goal and it will be so.**

Hatred cannot survive in a universe full of love.

**Happiness, that's success no matter where you are
or what your social status may be.**

Love life, you may just find it loving you right back.

**Love yourself, take time off for a vacation
or time to relax and just appreciate being.**

No one can tell you you're wrong for doing right,
yet do know your wrongs from rights.

When you have a good thing, keep it.

Never leave when you need to stay,
never stay when you need to leave.

Lead by example, inspire and influence.

This moment would not have existed if it be not for love,
and for to be blessed.

**When you know nothing, it was,
you know everything it is.**

Focus on and maintain healthy lifestyles,
cleanliness feels good.

**Do know and or learn the difference between good,
wholesome, healthy happiness and temporary pleasures
falsified by things such as addiction and unhealthy habits.**

Love and value good times,
especially those shared with friends and family.
Create the memories and cherish the moments.

Know inside yourself when and if you are or are not satisfied with something, including situations. Know what needs change and be content with that which does not.

Carry with you an appreciation of the time
that others have so chosen to give you.

Do choose to be mentally presently present in this moment. Hold with you not past negativities.

Know when you do not know, you do not know.

Question marks are great. What wonder would be wondered if all was known up under?

One of my lifetimes primary focuses is to expand
awareness, as well as open the hearts and minds of others.
To share my ideas and views for so to assist you
and enhance the expansion of love
and said ideas within others.

When you become a whole truth, you will then know.

Allow not your happiness to be stolen,
allow not your love to be tainted.
Allow not your image to be tarnished
and allow not your glow to be dimmed.

Have faith, in belief is strength.

Be gentle with children, they do not know what they do
not know. They too are works in progress.

**If you stick together, you'll never be lost.
Someone will always know exactly where you are.**

Avoid negative tendencies and habits, do promote,
influence, and encourage positive ones.

**Socialize, do learn one another as much as possible.
We each are uniquely created and have much blessings to
share with the world. Every person is meant to be a
positive addition to life and all that is.**

True is love.

**Limit not your imagination as it is
and be so with God all things are possible.**

Live love always and in all ways always.

You cannot have outer peace without inner peace.

To fight the fire of hatred,
use the love that flows as does water.

Sometimes our losses are our greatest gains.

If you do not like the direction of you're heading,
change or alter your course.

Love, is never against you.

You cannot fail at trying, that you either did or didn't do.

Judge not as it is less you become judged first. Choose not to criticize the efforts of others as they are in process of progress. Compare not your time line to those of others.

To share the gift of life with one another is the way.

For each is a pedestal and it is as so that yours can never be mine and mine can never be yours.

The world is your stage, and life is your audience.

Show worthiness of respect by giving such.

One can teach lesson through word, yet if one applies not
their own strategies and does not fully understand such,
they are difficulty learned when taught.

**When something is fully understood
it can be taught several ways.**

To show the way, walk the way.

**Everything should come full circle including
our procedures and processes.**

Know inside yourself, for every good given
is a contradiction of such or something that in some way
will attempt to minus it or from it.

**Learn to safeguard even the safeguards
without violating freedom, flexibility, or functionality.**

Do invent, reinvent, and innovate
to the point of either satisfaction or that which is
currently perceived as perfection for said object,
invention, process, or procedure.

Try not to make permanent decisions based upon temporary emotions.

Work is a virtue, and for such you'll find great reward.
For everything created, learned, gained,
or achieved is some type of resistance.
This builds strength and or stamina.

You cannot crush that which cannot be seen.

Always believe in you,
you were intentionally created as God said yes.

**Let not an at times a cruel world kill
or damage your kind spirit.**

If you're good and you know you're doing right,
do keep at it.

**Everyone has a purpose.
You are loved dearly and greatly appreciated.**

If everyone thought that they could not change or impact the world in a positive way the world would never change as it would forever remain the same or grow in the opposite of directions.

If at times looking at how far you have to go to achieve your goals is difficult or discouraging, just look at how far you've come.

Sometimes, all someone needs is a good friend with an open heart, and an ear to hear.

To reach, carry with you the light for so to illuminate.

One good friend is worth more than one million enemies.

**I do not believe in hateful souls.
I do however know that hurtful people exist.**

If you're going to shoot something and you're not hunting, let it be the hatred out of time.

Smile, it may come back like a boomerang.

Do build lasting relationships deeply rooted in honesty.

**When and or where words fall short,
being human does not.**

There's a star in the sky with your name on it.
Know this as it is fact.

**When by wearing a crown, an individual is humbled,
he or she is truly worthy of such.**

Sometimes it takes time to make time.
A real man takes the time to give time.

**Happiness cannot be falsified by substances
such as drugs and or alcohol as such is temporarily
inhibiting one's true self.**

One way to sort or solve perplexities
is to mentally reverse engineer them.

As working, moving systems governments can be viewed from a mechanical perspective and as such can be calibrated or adjusted with proper understanding of all technicalities involved.

When I do not know, I remember what I do know
and that is that with God all things are possible.

**When a boy runs not from his responsibilities
that boy is becoming a man.**

Parenting is like being a school bus driver.
The goal should always be the children's safe arrival.

**With all things, the truth of it existed first.
The truth was or be the love, the word,
and the knowledge of such that very much
so forms the reality, structure, or blueprint
of what is true of such.**

As wisdom comes with age, truth is wise.

You are a gift to life, existence, and to yourself.

If we all target life's negativities, if we all protect,
we all have in turn become victorious.

**The truth is undefeatable,
the false could never permanently
or in permanent manner successfully oppose it.**

At times the path may seem narrow,
yet it is as so that this very characteristic
keeps us safely together and holds us close.

**The false or that outside the will of the truth shall
collapse in time as it cannot withstand, endure, or survive
the physical reality of time itself. All false foundations
shall erode and or collapse as their structures are not
everlasting as such has not been placed by God.**

What is not placed by God or His love shall collapse
in time or cease to exist due to the fact that there are
technical flaws in the designs and structures of such as
such lacks His sight.

Loyalty, courage, bravery, and honor are royal terms. They are integral foundational truths that spring or come directly from He who created all who created. These terms are of Him.

One who is truthful in all his ways shall be true to he, true to they, and true to the environment in which he lives. He then therefore exists as a whole truth.

The truth is always self-evident upon inspection and thus also therefore cannot be penetrated or altered by the false in permanent manner.

That which is truthful and or of truth and understood as such can be simplified for so to be comprehended easily by others.

The truth can be simplified to an understandable extent, or placed in a variety of words that carry the same meaning when understood.

One of the greatest gifts of life is the ability to define or be defined. Thus, in a sense a child becomes in part the definition or defining of the parent's love.

If one is whole-hearted, and gravitates toward love and positivity one can travel, or navigate the path of life with great clarity.

Negativity in no way adds up to positivity without being converted. Meaning you cannot add negative to negative and equal positivity.

Negativity subtracts from life. Positivity adds to life and is therefore a major factor in loves victory.

Changing, altering, innovating, recreating, or relocating that which is suspected to be falsely placed may prove to be a difficult task without sufficient evidence for such claims.

One of many, a stepping stone to light and guide your path is the phrase right is right, wrong is gone.

For a king to be a king, he must have that of royalty in some way beside him or he may find he lacks kingdom. Any woman who carries herself as such will always be a queen.

In all ways and in every aspect, the path of positivity,
possibilities, and potential was laid before you,
yet the route remains undefined until you so
choose to take those steps or designate that route.

There are times that our paths are unclear and it is in such
times we must choose to walk by faith and not by sight.
We must choose to do that which feels right.

The turns we take and which way are of great
importance, however it is the direction of travel and that
it be positive that will forever be critical to our growth
both as one persons, and as one whole.

One becomes what is considered mature when mind,
body, and soul align and one also comes of age to handle
his or her responsibilities and tasks at hand accordingly.

Humanities state of consciousness or awareness represents
the sum of our general age and or growth. For example,
how woke is humanity? What is the current general level
of awareness and social consciousness of such. What is the
sum of all awareness, this determines humanities
mentality and maturity as one.

Always speak highly of oneself, regard and acknowledge
oneself with positivity. We are royalty.

For the curious, it is literally a matter of time or a sequence of thought or events before you understand you are of love.

Our inner truth is self-evident.

**He who created all knows every aspect of every perspective or angle ever forever.
From the depth of pain to the heights of happiness.**

He who created knows His creation well.

Do you know it is a technical truth that to exist you must be thought of? Nothing that exists does so without the thought of such existing first.

One who practices the purification of thought is elevating oneself in the direction of Heaven, as purity is of that which is Heavenly.

**The word can't, can simply mean not right now due to unforeseen, or un-understandable circumstances.
It is with God all things are possible.**

Everything God created comes full circle and is
purposeful. Life runs in cycles or circles.
That which we create should also come full circle
or for example be recyclable.

**When following the laws of love, life, and humanity from
an aerial perspective of all actuality so to speak creating
or structuring societies blueprint is a process of clarity.**

The easiest way to combat that which cannot be seen
is by loving that which can.

**Other than our creator, happiness in general holds the
highest value of all things. Happiness and the pursuit of
such both as individuals and as a whole is a basic,
essential and fundamental foundational value of life itself.
Our purpose in general is to prosper and to grow and to
be happy or to pursue such. Happiness can also be viewed
as the destination.**

To protect, preserve, ensure, and secure the positive
growth of the three including love, life, & humanity
should be the ultimate goal of all.

**If you safeguard the love, the life, and the humanity
you'll find solid foundation to build upon.**

Positive perception is key, our foundation will always have been love as such is more than the forever formula it is that which we are of. It is that which God is and therefore is always His first ingredient.

If you knew the infinitely positive value of a smile, you'd laugh, love it, and multiply that value as you share that moment with God.

Life is limitless, and time is of essence.

If you add time to the formulation of an idea and reference the current laws of life at that particular point in a period of forever anything is possible with God.

If you're going the wrong way, well, you're going the wrong way. Do go right even when you go left.

It is not truth that withstands the test of time, but time that withstands the test of truth as time was invented by the truth. God is love, in eternity first was the word as such had to be described or acknowledged that it so existed.

If a mans in love, he'll wrap those words around every detail of his love's life.

If he really loves you, he'll love loving you.

That which is too difficult to explain is
not thoroughly understood.

**Any positive route will eventually bring you
to a place of similar or the same.**

The destination will always be happiness,
yet it seems the trick is to make that of this journey.

Happiness holds an infinitely positive value.

One need only know all was nothing to appreciate
all that is.

**If you'd like a before and after photo of life,
close and open your eyes.**

The love that is would not be if not be for the love that is.

The door that closed on hatred, has opened for love.

If you wish to create something successful
add your love to its formula.

**In every moment rests opportunity yet every opportunity
is not of loves, is not of truths.**

In hatreds shallows many negatives can be found.
Among them jealousy and envy.

**If you so choose to kill or corrupt or destroy that which
is, you have so chosen to give your enemy the breath of
life. In that moment your enemy becomes victorious for
the time being.**

Sometimes it is not how we look at things so much that
matters, but how we see things. Perception is key.
How do you perceive that which surrounds you?
How do you choose to view the situation?

When I see, I see life. When I look, I find depth of detail.

A glimpse of God's goodness is sure to awaken
the same goodness within us.

Anyone is capable of temporarily losing. Its simplified definition is not trying. Even in a loss something can be gained or learned and therefore there's no such thing as a loss unless said loss is fatal then it be not such or is therefore non-existent to he who perseveres.

Travelling through time negativity is past or present
tense while positivity is the present or future tense or
projection of what life could or should be.
Meaning negativities should be behind us,
while we look forward to a positive future.

**Conquer today's world with understanding
and you'll find it was already yours.**

When you're at peace with the world
you'll receive more than a piece of the world.

**God knew or could calculate or predict
your current thoughts before time began.**

Sometimes we feel we have to at least check
left before going right,
yet it's only a matter of time
before we go right.

**Sooner is much better than later,
yet still later is better than never.**

Be proud of yourself.
If God placed anyone else in your shoes they would fail.

**Some rivers run wild. While the words to the word,
the very truth itself flows freely through my heart.**

Allow not the false to provide or be the source of your
happiness as you will be led astray from the love of truth.

**One of our most common beliefs is in goodness.
Humans by nature will always gravitate
toward the source of their happiness.**

Love is logical.

If anything travels faster than light, it's darkness.

Sometimes the smallest details can hold
the greatest or grandest significance.

**If I could give to you anything,
it would be understanding.**

There is always a way to get there,
but there's no point in going alone.

Love is trusted, and trusted is love with truth.

If it opened your mind,
I was right even when or if I was wrong.

**A glimpse of light many times can alter
your whole thought process or way of thinking.**

Anger is the result of a fool's frustrations
while a genius finds a different approach
to conquering their problems or issues at hand.

**One day, the fake will get tired of being false
and the truth will remain the same.**

There's a junction in time where man's reality aligns
with that which God had intended, and most of us merge
right if we had not done so at a previous point in time.

**Embrace your positive self. You'll find it quite satisfying
when you let go of all the negativity.**

I chose to live and to breathe to serve His purpose for me
and not my own. It's really that simple.

**If the words are present in my mind,
and I know them to be either truth or link to such
I would be a fool not to speak or to write them.**

While the devil's hatred is a confusion of anger,
God's fury is focused intelligence.

It's difficult to walk a straight path through a dark forest.

Recognizing negativities, possibilities, or the problematic
areas or points in time is critical to our survival.
Half the battle is locating said battles.

**The quality of our lives can be altered or adjusted
by perfecting the lines drawn through time or by
adjusting that which is variable to provide flexibility.
Meaning some laws are set in stone while others are not.
Do know and understand this.**

God's laws, will always be written in stone.

**When my life is over, I can honestly say I did my best
and gave it my all. Blood, sweat, and tears.**

It would be foolish to set in stone that which may need to
be changed or altered at later points in time.
An open mind rapidly grows and evolves.

**As a man who is becoming rather wise in his ways
and had to grow, and learn the world I know, recognize,
and acknowledge the foolishness of my past.**

Mistakes many times are mistaken for failures when in all actuality they are stepping stones to success.

One day I woke up to something strangely familiar, something I knew I knew.

Strength is not something I have. It is one of my core ingredients and therefore it is that which I am of.

From the deepest depth, to the highest height, from everything within or of me I thank you.

May the voice of love be forever heard and felt throughout humanities minds, hearts and souls.

If sorting technicalities it is of wisdom to utilize your practical, logical intellectual self rather than base your decisions upon emotion.

When darkness is behind us,
when we emerge from our dark era's and awaken
we will see clearly a beautiful bright future.

Unity does not mean conformity, nor does it feel restricting. Simplified it could mean we're all headed the same direction via various different paths.

A good parent, will find what his child loves to do or would like to do and see to it that it be done in a safe positive way or not done at all.

When you seek and search for or find the truth, hold it and never let it go.

When someone loves you, all the negative in the world couldn't shatter or tarnish their positive image of you.

Though I claim a direction of travel to be the one, I have but only my life to live and would not live yours for you even if I could.

In a sense my strength is of ancient origin and my love is everlastingly new.

The reality of tomorrows outcome is based upon one's own understanding of such.

If I ceased my efforts to deliver you the truth,
or to deliver you from that which is evil
I would have to diagnose myself as suicidal.
I would never present you with a false love.

**At the beginning of each new day,
I feel somewhat refreshed as if the painful stains of past yesterdays have vanished and I begin new.
Every day is a new start, a fresh chance to begin anew.**

Do you wholeheartedly do that which you do?
Your soul knows if you are lying.

Forming judgement or final determination is for the closed minded. Closing one's mind is similar to the suicide of mental development as it is opposite of growth. It is as if one has closed the book on oneself or another and or ceased growth.

If you surround yourself with love and truthful genuine people the quality of your life will vastly improve.

**The trick to navigating time and creating the life one wishes to have, is to make the present resemble future positivity and not the negativity of the past.
In doing so you alter your course and control your destiny while designing your destination.**

Have you ever been someone's everything?
You've always been.

**Life is love placed in a timeline and defined to an impossibly possible extent while expressing itself and defining what it is and shall be. Life is the defining undefinable infinity. Life is an expression.
Life is love expressed in an experience.**

Truth comforts, settles one's mind and rests ones worries.

**There is no such thing as a hater later in time.
Right now, they're just confused and cannot translate their own emotions.**

Being in love gives you a direction to channel your positive energy, omnipresence comes to mind.

**You will find love, from here to its furthest reach.
You are loved.**

I know I knew, but wouldn't know until sunrise,
I must have kissed her goodnight.

Love loves love. It is forever and always all enduring.

Anytime true and false collide,
it is but a matter of time before truth remains.

Your smiles worth the world, and the wait.

If God was light, He would say I love you this much.

**Love could be described yet not defined
as a very satisfying unsatisfiable need to satisfy
and care for in all ways love and therefore is everlasting.**

When in love, one feels fulfilled yet it is continuously
in motion or existing as such on a timeline
and therefore is forever.

**Love is never ending, everlasting, self-driven
and continuous. The joy of its existence is in existing
and as so is the forever formula.**

If you love her, you'll go as many extra miles as it takes to show and express that love and you'll also enjoy yourself in doing so.

I wish to murder your fears, kill your negativity and crush your limits by way of love.

Love messages cannot be lost in translation as they speak for themselves.

The truth, will never be a lie.

While running against the wind,
it is fact one will be met with resistance.
Wise is to travel in the same direction as love.

**Sorting out all actuality in all actuality
is actually a matter of but not limited to practicality
and technicality involving mathematics**

To straighten that which has been made crooked,
an alignment is necessary.

**To be a parent is to be your child's best friend
and to always be a source of inspiration, assistance,
and positivity in all ways, always.**

Practicality is technical true probability
or likeliness that an event or action can be formulated
or placed successfully into physical reality.

**Technicality can be used as a tool to eliminate
false possibility from consideration.**

Life's design is really quite systematic. Truth is logical.

**It is not so much about making peace
as it is about living peace.
To be at peace or have peace,
one must become that.**

The key to your heart is locked in your heart
so that only you can find it.
Nothing can take that from you.

**Life is a beginning that knows no end,
and love is everything in between.**

What is all to he who has nothing?
As a matter of fact, everything is a matter of time.

**Standing straight can also be considered moving forward.
Sometimes to be established is to be aware of the reality of oneself.**

Did anybody thank you for being you? He did.

Hate has an ugly ring to it, loves a beautiful song.

If you can find success in all ways
it betters success in someways always.

**Not only was royalty established, it was realized.
It was brought to life from within via the awakening.**

Though evil may temporarily blind or wound you,
he who loves heart holds strong wherever his love may be.

Every detail; from the depth of thought to imaginations height is life.

Truth cannot be stolen from truth, and can only be given and therefore will always be whole in its entirety. Truth is not incomplete.

I'll pursue your happiness until every drop of life is but the sweetest joy.

If you wish to know God's thoughts, gather that which is known of wisdom; for link to Him, rests inside yourself.

When all that is to be glorious is victorious the glory of God shall be known.

When reals really real fake is quite transparent.

Failure is only possible if one's brain temporarily believes in the existence of such.

Nothing's impossible, but some things are not
of possibility yet as the path to the way
has not been paved in a physical reality.

**One can unlock positivity's potential
by reducing negativities probability.**

Because He who knew knows what's knowns
unknown new news no. Senseless sense,
it's a fancy way of saying trust God knows.

**As time be living link to truth, truth be living in time,
and this moment, is real.**

His joy, is for the love of His joy,
or one could say His joy, is Love.

**God' s fury is a very focused, concentrated intelligence,
be not confused with the confusion of negativity.**

Hell hath no wrath like God' s fury and truth
need not be fortified as it is fully in definition.

**Negativity is a past nightmare that in time fades
as a glorious day is born.**

When one finds the direction to channel that of love
and the appreciation of such the heart races.

If it was not for the love of love, be it why?

I love seeing that of royalty wearing their crowns well,
it's an Honor to witness such beauty.

Perfection is a question of one's perception.

Key is to subtract negativity and add positivity
thus increasing positive possibilities probability.

Love works, try that.

A dream is yet a dream if the path to such
is not physically paved.

Every success was once a decision.

Love loves the hell out of love. True story.

**If an obvious truth loses debate,
a common reason would be lack of clarification
via communication; or presence of darkness.**

The truth, can serve as both shield and sword.

The beauty of loving is in loving, and in so many ways.

If one's heart is truly taken, one's mind,
body and soul will be as well.

If you love her, you'll learn sign language.

My heart can't be broken, I gave everyone a piece of it.

One of my only fears, my love in the hands of hate.

Truth can be your elevator. In that sense I think we all pick the top floor for the view. Life is beautiful.

In / with all positivity every opinion of immeasurable value, with God through communication anything is possible.

With God through communication anything is possible.

**Every woman's heart has a door,
they either open it or close it for you,
real men respect that decision always.**

If I thought not of future thought
I fought not for a future sought.

**He of wisdom falls not blindly for one's body,
but clearly for heart and soul.**

It is of wisdom to invest in tomorrow's today.

**Loyalty is to place love over one's own ambitions
lead by temptations and is of royalty.**

I like to launch little love missiles at hate through time.
It's my new hobby.

He didn't break your heart, smile he fortified it.

One need look no further than oneself to find truth,
it is that which you are of.

A loving life encourages a love of life.

Wrong to fight fire with fire,
what about upping loves water pressure?

**Really hate is inevitably self-destructive
in nature as hate even hates hate.**

Love loves love hate hates even hate,
one is forever, one simply is not.

**Here today, gone tomorrow,
but when I leave, I left you me.**

Truth is eternal and that of such cannot be killed.

You can only lie to truth for a limited time.

I thought about you till my thoughts thought about you.

**Even though right is right
I'll be wrong but right till right is right.**

When earths evil be defeated,
the Heavens shall sing of the sweetest joy.

**Ever seen a peaceful warlord?
Be not confused your enemy is in hiding.**

When all be one, all be won.

You can count me out until the day you count you in.

You deserve every detail.

**Pursing positivity multiplies possible positive potential,
maximize that while minimizing negativity
in a forward motion.**

d.r.u.g.s. = dumb reason you're going stupid.

**If you proceed not with love,
your process be not progressive.**

In a way I ran through a forest of many obstacles
and made a path to many pleasures.

**Blessed I be if blessing it be even if said blessing
is me or mine, preferably it be yours.**

Dreams are the seeds of reality,
please do align with that of positivity.

**The act of increasing positivity's probability
reduces negativities possibility,
and by doing so, it's a forever formula.**

How can ones heart be so in love with where it not be?

**My heart fell in a wishing well and wishes it well.
Does that make any sense right now?**

She is my infinity defined.

**As a child I told myself the stars could hear my wishes,
I still believe it to be true.**

Dear love, please stop launching Satan's hate missiles
at me. thank you, love.

**When she smiles, I say di di di did you just smile cause my
flutter just flickered.**

In the beginning, the truth knew the end; in the end, it
isn't the end but the understanding of the beginning.

The only thing more important than right now is right now.

This is a hell of a crime scene, hate, your guilty.

Searching possible contradictions one can find agreement.

I wish to love the life with the love of my life.

If I ever stand for anything other than love, I hope love knocks me down to open my eyes.

If He's really the master, He'll let you shine.

Always trust friends, if you cannot trust them, they're not friends.

Reveal your intentions, secrecy is of evil.

Always explain thoroughly and state all that is necessary.

Little depends on reputation, establish oneself as good.

Appreciate attention, yet find unnecessary.

Serve others whenever possible, in itself is reward.

Cater to others if possible.

Provide thorough truth whenever possible.

Cure: Embrace the unhappy and unlucky.

Learn to teach people interdependence.

If you have or are looking for victims, you're travelling in the wrong direction. See God for details.

Falsify no truth; ask in all honesty if help is needed.

Develop strong healthy friendships based on honesty.

Learn conversions. You can crush not,
that which cannot be seen.

Use presence to show worthiness of respect and honor.

Hell hath no wrath like Gods fury. Nothing is unpredictable when you know everything is possible.

Fortify your fortress and send invitations.

Send not false threats as they may be mistaken for truth.

Invest in life, yet do know your physical limitations.

The elevation and enlightenment of all in a period of forever is a never-ending path through time.

Share in all honesty truths and convert negative energy or emotion by enlightening.

Concentration of force may create imbalances.

Only truth or a truth can stand the test of time.

It is possible to in certain aspects re-invent who you are or will become, yet it is He who created all who created who created you.

Does a shepherd not dirty His own hands and feet if necessary to assist His sheep?

You cannot fortify falsities against truth as it is truth is written in stone.

Boast not, for in such equation may be arrogance.

The wise guy seen before the smart ass saw.
Only God knows the beginning and end of all things.

Share your wins and losses to encourage and promote the victories of others.

Allow as many options as possible to provide flexibility and freedom of choice.

Create not false hope, as it is God who knows your true intent, and theirs.

Invest in the happiness of others, you will find yourself greatly rewarded.

Royalty is to be and shall be established.

Time is of essence, Patience is a virtue yes. Perfected knowledge is also more than a concept.

**Harbor not negativity:
See the law of attraction for details.**

Your thoughts become your reality; do be Royal in your ways.

**Notice the fisherman awaits his catch,
even if in pursuit of such.**

Learn when to be content,
and graciously accept the free lunch if needed.

**Be yourself. You are great.
You are unique, you are a miracle.**

Strike the shepherd, expect lightning.

**Invest and assist in the positive growth of the hearts
and minds of all.**

A friend is worth more than an enemy.
Learn conversions.

Share truth and behold, truth be told for so to see clearly.

God is perfect in all His ways.

Heaven will always be the destination.

No form is unformed, even that which is like water has been formed as such.

Always be truthful in your ways.

Honesty is the best policy.

Be true to oneself.

Be true to one another.

Be true to one's environment.

Never proceed with negative intent.

Always care.

Try not to not try.

Be non-judgmental.

Form not conclusion in absence of fact.

Do form positive tendency.

Never lose hope, it is with God all things are possible.

Do be like water.

Never make permanent decisions
based upon temporary emotion.

**Do be fast to forgive,
yet remember that which is necessary.**

Patience is a virtue, yes. and time is precise.

Listen to your heart yet do censor with rational thought.

Criminal intent is punishable by law.

Happiness is essential and cannot be falsified.

The honest intent of innocence shall always be protected.

Only God can create soul, see God for details.

Love loves to love loved love to love love.

You are unique, there is and will be no other like you.

You are similar, we are all human beings.

**The key to your heart is in your heart
so only you can find it.**

Never lie to your love, again honesty is the best policy.

Karma is a beauty, she cannot be manipulated.

Your intent was, is and always will be known.

**Only the man who made the rock,
can pull the sword from the stone.**

Prayer is powerful, please do ask if and when in need.

Everything happens for a reason.

Behind every smile is a truth,
behind every frown is a contradiction.

Rush not that which is yet to be understood.
Patience is a virtue.

Only God knew the beginning and end of all things.

Give what you wish to receive
to receive what you wish to get.

**To do away with hatred,
spread the love that flow like water.**

If it be not for love it not be.

**It's hard to get everyone on the same page
if they're not reading from the same book.**

If a world of falsities prevents that of truth
from breathing life, I left you this.

**If you defeat the evil in your own masculinity / femininity
and give the ball to God, He may have surprises for you.**

You may not always like the truth,
but in a million years it's still the truth.

**There were a couple interceptions,
but the home team always had better reception.**

If He doesn't believe the truth,
He will believe the false for a limited time.

**I could tell you the same things
you will tell yourself in time.**

Your blueprint is inevitable, your destiny is to be happy.

**Master your mind-state and you may find yourself
key to yourself.**

Ever throw water at hellfire through time?
Love is, was and always will be love.

**When I see her; my inner in awe awes in all honesty,
I am all-in-all in awe.**

I win some, lose some but we as one won.

Let not the false of the day affect the truth inside it.

Sometimes I draw conclusions from others work,
yet mainly I use my own reference points.

**He of the wise be not lustful, but of love,
and passion, and truth.**

I wish I could wrap the words I love you
around every aspect of your life.

I found myself lost in love.

Type Heaven into the search bar, you see a path or steps to light; a path of light can also be seen as a path or elevated motion to truth.

Love is a universal language.

In sight was, is and always will be an infinity of happiness.

There is a language of passion softly spoken, not to be confused with words.

Wish I could tell you if it wasn't, you're safe now.

Perfect isn't perfect perfect is perfect.

If I was a walking talking heart, I'd fall apart seeing you and put myself back together to see you again before you noticed it happened.

Love can make a man submit in all ways always, even in his heart his own masculinity. undeniable attraction.

When I see her, I lose myself and become a living expression of God's love.

**Just the thought of her love makes me dizzy.
Can't. Hold. Thoughts.**

My soul needs, my body wants, and my mind likes, she's it and it could be defined as love.

**All women are beautiful,
yet she redefines the word every time I see her.**

My heart fell a couple times but it got back up.

A beautiful thing = love, life, & humanity.

Many times, attitude is the difference between a good day
and a bad day.

I would have never been me if I never met you.

Some of the best lessons in life
you learn yourself with God.

**Sometimes you learn what's right by learning / knowing
what's wrong.**

Seemingly as strong as the truth itself,
her love endures forever.

She is not temporary.

To solve a perplexity, sort by criticality, then resolve
issues using common logic and technicalities.

**Any complex situation can be simplified in time by
understanding or continued pursuit of understanding.**

Life isn't a sprint, nor a marathon,
it is the walk that is most enjoyable.

**You can do, and you can achieve anything
your heart desires.**

You are much more amazing than amazing will ever be.

**Love; goes around, comes back around,
and always will. God Bless you.**

Trust yourself, and always strive for what's right.

**In a maze of ways, right isn't always right,
yet always go right.**

Wisdom can be found in still waters,
as thoughts can be developed in time.

**If I stop telling you I love you,
you might forget.**

From there to Heaven an everyone in between,
thank you.

What it is, and was once but a dream.

To be great is to inspire greatness.

**Searching possible contradictions
one can find agreements.**

Any positive path will lead to a destination of the same.

A good friends joy is your happiness.

To be or say one is of wisdom is wise
while to say one is wise is foolish.

**Time doesn't stop, and whether you're with it
or against it, it always wins.**

Carry with you your love where ever it is you go.

**You won't find today's page in yesterday's book.
We're reading from the future now.**

Through all it's been through your love never died,
I'm proud of you.

**It hurts when you invest your all in a relationship,
and their all doesn't come back.**

When truth wash away what lies, love remains.

**Is it that one's own judgment need be judged
until such is just?**

Sometimes, what someone doesn't say means
more than what they did.

It's not that your wrong, but that it isn't right.

Follow me but follow me not,
better yet follow the truth inside oneself.

**A good leader feels only as accomplished
as the last of whom he leads.**

Life is sign language for I Love You.

**Life is the real, true, physical translation
or expression of love.**

Focus fully on positivity and fortify your positive self.

Even he who is right can be wrong sometimes.

Ladies; if you don't know if he loves you or not,
odds are he don't.

**I believe not in death,
for it is the last of the lies you'll find.**

To stop the violence, we as one must attack the birthplace
of such hatred. Our children are the future.

**Always promote and encourage healthy lifestyles
and the growth of positivity.**

False tried to bury itself in truth,
and well, it got buried. all in time.

**Yesterday wasn't a loss,
it was the step that put victory in sight.**

Incoming information or knowledge is harmful
when misunderstood in the wrong hands.

**Please do monitor that which your child witnesses
in all ways always.**

It is a matter of destroying the hatred that's destroying
us, or becoming at the least a victim of such hatred.

**Thank God for the birth of every child,
it is in their eyes I see my future.**

Locating the battlefield is half the battle.
Every time you'll find it somewhere in time.

Negativities must be strategically fought and prevented.

You can promote a healthy subconscious by consciously
encouraging and promoting healthy lifestyles.
Today's seeds bloom tomorrow.

**One's reality in all actuality is a combination of what is,
and how one perceives that which is. think positive.**

It is not of possibility for an obstacle to be in all ways
greater than that which encounters it.

**Love is both the destiny and destination,
it is also with whom you share your present.**

There is no doubt in my mind, without the love of God,
I wouldn't be here today.

**If one wishes to succeed tomorrow,
one must first learn how today.**

Two of the most powerful if not the most powerful forces
in the universe are positivity and negativity;
you draw the conclusions.

**It's hard when you know what's right and people won't
let or allow you to do what's right.
They try to tell you how to be you. Time heals all.**

To speak of the unknown,
or unproveable one must risk humiliation.

**I'm used to my love humiliating me,
my life has become quite the comedy.**

If I focused on pain I would cry forever, instead I'll pick
you up an we'll cry together when we find forever.

**If my mind was separate from my body,
I would never leave you.**

You'll never know what someone's been through
to be them.

**One can let life's negativities bring them down,
or allow them to serve as the contrast that gave direction
and elevated oneself.**

In time you will understand what you didn't understand,
and that is what you won't understand until you
understand. Trust, God knows.

**It is truth you fight fire with water,
and truth flows freely as does water.**

I strongly believe that any given situation can be tackled
with common logic if oneself is centered in that which is
of the truth of love.

**I have a tendency to delete myself when considering most
matters. Personal opinion is but an irrelevance.
It is the truth I seek to find.**

Retaliation is a double negative,
why lower yourself to a level similar to that of hatred?

Sometimes wrong answers guide us to the right ones as we learn from our mistakes.

If you can, place a love of life in your heart and keep it there. Let nothing take that from you.

**A lie can only live so long,
there around for a limited time only.**

Any human being knows what all human beings need, that's how I know you know you know.

**Success is not how you bless yourself,
it's how you bless those you love or care about.**

Even a positive thought or words of encouragement is an investment in your future.
Sometimes it's all we have to give.

Express yourself. Positively.

Creative expression is how we channel imagination.

**Change is inevitable, though the direction of growth
is sometimes an option.**

One could say it is possible to wrap different words
around the same truth several ways.
If said truth is understood.

**Whatever you do, do it with all of you,
your mind, body and soul.**

Healthy mind + healthy body + healthy soul
= healthy you.

Dream your dreams right into reality.

Hope is that which is held for something for
or of the future, always hope for something.

I'm an artist, I arrange words around simple truths in an articulate manner.

Positivity is powerful, negativity is as well.

I would not advise investing that of negativity into life, really its bad math.

When you value yourself and have self-respect, the world takes notice.

Your worth every details detail of it.

If we all help, we all we all win.

A smile can change the world.

Whatever be thought of,
let even the very thought of it be beautiful.

My thoughts and prayers are with you, always.

I give of myself to give God the breath of life through me,
wherever it be I live, He too lives as well.

Let not emotion overcome rational thought.

Ever evaluate your path through life?
Turn a dream into a destination?

Different life, different calculation.

It's not that I know its definition,
but that I know in all that's defined it exists.

If I could fill the word grateful with grateful it still wouldn't be as grateful as I feel I am. thank you.

Somehow, somewhere in time life is picture perfect,
and the picture is perfect.

If you're a thinker almost any thought or idea can spark or begin a sequence of thoughts that leads to a positive outcome or conclusion.

I am determined and to be determined
is my continuous destiny.

**I'm enjoying the journey or one could say
I am happily in process of progress.**

To encourage the formation of healthy thought patterns,
promote and encourage healthy lifestyles.
Love, love, & happiness.

**Every thought a spark, every spark a link
to an idea or concept.**

Don't invest in stress, it's a time trap.

**Problems are like rubix cubes, the right combination
of turns / thoughts and bam, there it is.**

If my physical ability matched my hearts will to help you,
God knows I would move mountains in your favor
if need be.

**Even if I provoke the thought that provokes the thought
of the thought, I have fulfilled my purpose.**

Many times, I reach for truth with no specific target
in mind, my only motivation is to help.

**If stress is a factor in your thought process
try relaxing and reformulating them.**

He of wisdom knows wisdom can be found in all places.

I think your purpose on earth is to fulfill your destiny, and I think part of fulfilling your destiny is finding your positive happiness.

Did I tell you love's a boomerang?
It'll always come back sometime in time.

It's not a question of why, it's a question of why not.

I'm convinced if it didn't work then it was because this wasn't this and that wasn't that.

If odds were against us, we wouldn't be.

Set no limitations and break through all barriers with an open mind and heart.

God's belief in you is endless.

The only doors I close lead to trouble.

Of all the things I would consider myself, above all I would say is a student. I will never fully quench my thirst for knowledge or wisdom.

If you make not a conscious effort to do that of good, you may unknowingly be doing just the opposite.

Anything possible is possible.

The truth of human nature has a way of finding itself in time.

If a situation cannot be simplified or understandably clarified by all parties involved allow time if possible to sort out contradictions.

Learn to work the clock and form estimations based on projected growth.

In every second of every moment, you have the choice to form decisions that will shape your future.

Proper assessment of any situation is critical to forming a resolution.

**I'm the opposite of gullible,
I'm forever grateful but still don't believe my eyes.**

Woman are like roses, real pretty.
But can be painful.

**God likes you for you, and he'd like it a lot
if you'd like you for you too.**

God is the one you can turn your glow off for,
and he'll still see your shine.

**Ever have a heart to heart with someone who loves you,
you're living one.**

**Live not in conflict of your nature,
yet do know what is not of such.**

God is powerful, as is His love.

Trust in God, and answers will come.

When in doubt ask Jesus, He is God's Son.

**Theoretically speaking pulling is better than pushing,
do pull do not push.**

Life's good, do go right even if you go left.

Don't hate, appreciate.

Celebrities aren't objects or little lights
that blink for our amusement,
there people we need to respect and appreciate.

**If you knew your value or significance,
you'd probably want some bubble wrap.**

Our children are human beings not human bodies.

**Often parents care for their child's physical well-being
rather than consciously nurturing also the mental,
physical, and spiritual whole.**

Every life is a precious, very delicate situation.

**On a light note, have a blessed day.
I hope it shows you how beautiful life really is or can be.**

Ever love to love and be loved love in love?
It is to be joyful.

**Too bad a minute can't tell you
to what extent one's hearts effort is invested.
Or how much passion is placed in artistic expression.**

There is something about art I will forever appreciate.

**Note to self; the man behind the hand that holds the pen
cannot save the world with word alone.**

I wish there was an alarm clock to
awaken and give rise to the truth within.
So that they who can know, they are of love.

**May God hold, and bless your hearts for to comfort.
My thoughts and prayers are with you always.**

Thank you, for being you. and with those words
I write in time what will forever rest in memory
a moment of appreciation.

**If the world isn't yours in time, your heart may be in the
wrong location or traveling in the wrong direction.**

When you surrender yourself to love,
you become it and gain the world.

A smile is a positive event in time, and there fun to share.

Sometimes I wonder if there is a proper formula
or proper way to form thoughts,
and maybe I know an unknown secret of such.

**If I could choose to be good, better, or best,
I'd pick good to have much life left getting better
while being overseen by the best.**

I think of all things I am most fascinated
with the very thought of a thought or idea
or with thinking or thought in general. Depth.

**In the beginning, life is question; in the end,
life is answers.**

I tend to believe you have no weaknesses,
your strengths being compared creates an illusion of such.

Ever watch woman with style?
It isn't what she has its how she wears what she has
and her smiles her best feature.

If a case is never defined, form no judgment.

In a world where everyone develops or forms personal opinion an elevated or enlightened one shares perspective.

The very essence or formula for such of an individual
is only known by God and can be fully understood
or comprehended by no human being.

**A willingness to be open-minded and share perspectives
is key to reaching common understanding.**

It wouldn't be of wisdom to skip a and b on your way to c.

**Any pre-planned action / motion through time started
as an idea formulated into a physical process such
as instructions / blueprints.**

Love is lawed. Lawed is love.

**Part of growth is learning
how to utilize all available knowledge.**

Life is going through a process of purification.

**I prayed once, the length of said prayer
was my entire life.**

Not wise is to criticize that which you yet not understand until a thorough investigation of theories, variables, facts, and technicalities.

**If we realized or understood to an extent the criticality
of the moves we make in time, some of us would think
twice the first time.**

You make me want to witness all that is, which is you.

**If I could think a thought that would help you think
a thought then I thought a thought of thoughtfulness.**

The most dominate force in the universe will always
be love and or positivity.

**If you grow, surely you were born and created and are
loved as hates own nature wouldn't allow such.**

Every piece of information in the universe can be viewed
as some type of reference point.

**To find a light switch in a dark room one begins
by searching all physical surfaces starting
with that which is the most likely of places.**

Forever is possible if it's possible.

**An infinite search of all possible mentality, physicality,
and spirituality would lead to infinite results
or combinations of such.**

Part of life is enjoying enjoyment when you find yours.

Ever center yourself?
Please if so, allow it to be in that of love.

Sometimes I sit back and spend time appreciating or enjoying depth of detail.

Only God knows the power of one, and the power of negativities on one. In all ways be positive.

I hate by loving the hell out of life.

My love is that which provides my sense of fulfillment and makes me complete.

God leaves or abandons not the truth, we do or did.

**When you really find yourself,
you'll find God right there waiting for you.**

Thank you to those who recognize the power of love,
and of positivity.

**Forcing change is formula for failure,
however understanding the nature of something
and adding positive influence can redirect growth.**

Be content with that which is in or has a positive
or neutral state, understand the nature of change,
and apply love where necessary.

**Enjoy the journey of life with the spirit of adventure
all the way to happiness.**

Picture or visualize if you will a positive trip through
time, then make your dreams reality.

**Smile, laugh, love, live, relax,
if it's okay with you in time it's all good.**

Key is to love the love of the life that is,
while dreaming of the life that will be.

**I wouldn't consider revenge a success,
the success would be justice.**

I consider a mastermind someone who has mastered one's
own mentality or mind-state.

**Observation is one of a genius's favorite powers
or abilities.**

Contrast and contradiction can be used as tools
to sort true from false.

**One can learn some wisdom from watching
or observing one object, person, place or situation,
yet it is in all things all wisdom is found.**

Is your soul healthy? mind? body? are you winning?

That of a full truth or a truthful answer to a negative situation is never a negative solution and has always that of a positive outcome.

Rest the body, and soothe the soul to find peace of mind.

Have faith and rest assured, you are a peace to the plan. You do belong, this is your place.

My definition of to serve justice is to clarify and resolve in just manner, a just manner is that which does not over exercise the power or ability of authority and seeks an agreeably positive resolution for all parties involved.

That which is not right is not just.

May the path of love be paved forever more. God bless.

**Did anybody thank you for being you?
I did, and if you didn't, I wish you would too.
Spend a moment appreciating yourself.**

Does life have self-esteem? Is it that knowledge is power.

**Always try to follow a path of positivity,
let the loving life live life and love life.**

Whatever be done, let it be done lightheartedly lest it be
of justice then be done wholeheartedly. smile, have fun.

**It is possible to with clarity remove the negativity
from life in time, target it, counter and reverse it.**

Technically mistakes can happen, growth can as well.

Today I would be not a better me if not wished to be.

A dream is the visualization your hope and determination
can bring to life.

When you find and apply yourself, anything is possible.

All ways believe and have faith in love,
life, and happiness.

**Allow not that of negativity to manipulate your present,
life is what together we make it.**

One who knows what life could be,
and knows its current state could in a way assist
in its positive growth or evolution.

**Raising awareness and the multiplying of positivity
increases and strengthens life's defenses.**

Foolish is foolproof if said fool be the fool for love.

**Understanding isn't just a concept it is as a way of life
to live by. To understand when we don't understand
is understanding in itself.**

It is together, anything is possible.

Together, we can place in the past, past negativities and breathe life to our dreams.

Together we can make reality that which is known capable or possible of life's positive potential.

If you love her, you'll learn sign language.

Time heals all wounds and exposes all falsities.

Love love.

Help where, when, and if you can. Live and let live.

In every difficulty rests a simplified solution.

God didn't say we wouldn't make mistakes,
it was evil that said we would fail.

It is that what's not written is lost.

Master yourself, do practice patience and self-control.

**Mentally place yourself in a position of power.
Do you help and build that which lasts?
Or do you corrupt, destruct, and destroy?**

Do halt negativities as soon as possible.

Utilize knowledge known to advance.

The wise guy seen before the smart-ass saw.

**Life should be a parade of positivity
marching through time.**

I saw what I saw until I seen,
and upon being seen it was understood.

**To be or become positive is quite possibly
the most important decision you will ever make.**

Forever is possible if it's possible, it is not impossible.

**I wonder if life had self-esteem would it be high
or low at this particular point in time?**

To attack life's negativities up-root the instances of such situations. Attack evils breeding grounds with love.

Target, counter, and reverse negativities. Rip them out of your future by recognizing them in your past and present.

Do recognize the power of negativity, and the power of negativity on one's mind. Always think positive.

Write your own story, live your dream.

Never cage the imagination,
yet do recognize the difference between positive
and negative thought patterns.

Make healthy decisions, choose to think positive.

Lead a healthy lifestyle and choose to live life
to the fullest.

**He or she who risked not is yet to live.
Try new things, life has much to offer and explore.**

Hold onto happiness, its value is infinite.

Mentality is key, finding proper perspective.

Always believe in you, you are greater than any obstacle you will encounter.

Do minimize negative events in time as much as humanly possible.

What's best for you may not be best for me.

To understand you don't understand when you don't understand is understanding in itself.

There's nothing more beautiful than the smile in a child's eyes.

Never lose faith, always believe.

Never forget, yet do be quick to forgive.

Worry not, yet do work towards positive resolutions.

Pace yourself, patience is a virtue.

**I try to be thorough, complete in my teachings
I simplify the complex.**

One need not a dictionary of words to explain
that which is understood.

**When everything around you seems to be flustered,
that's when its most important to remain focused.**

Wisdom rests in still waters, settle the thoughts and relax the mind as you find within yourselves the answers to tomorrows questions.

You are limitless, you are incredibly gifted with the opportunity to be you and to create the best version of you can.

Today's choices lead to tomorrow's outcomes.

Sometimes it's easier to let go than to hold on, yet many times the easy thing isn't the right thing to do.

Never allow outside sources to affect your inner peace, or inhibit your positive potential in any situation.

I would be not a better me, if not wished to be.

The underlying reason I'm me or am like this is because I took the time to be, I wished to better myself.

**Beauty is in the eye of the beholder,
and that which is viewed as perfection depends
upon one's own perception of such.**

I firmly believe in the beauty of humanity,
and with such being said that we are all beautiful
and unique in our own distinct ways.

**If you so choose to judge someone based solely by where
they have been, you may very well miss where
that person is going.**

Dream, aspire, believe, do & become. Share, inspire, give,
receive and you'll see we've won.

**We know not what it took to make each other
and as so we should be not so quick to trample
on the hearts of one another.**

With these minds, and these hearts, and these hands,
look what we have accomplished.

**As I sat in traffic one day I realized, we care about each
other a lot more than we acknowledge at times.**

We should celebrate each other's existence,
and in doing so share appreciation of each other's
company and companionship.

**Sometimes we think we know what we want,
but it's in those times we must trust God and know
that He knows what we need.**

When I thought I knew what I wanted,
He knew what I needed.

As a person you cannot be broken, only fortified.

We all fall sometimes, it's how you handle it
and how you get back up that matters most.

It's a lot easier to be good, than to do bad.

Never let someone tell you your dreams are too big
to achieve, aim for the stars.

We're all stars, we just shine different.

Be not selfish in your ways, invest your time in your loves.

**Appreciate and value the time others choose to give you,
that is something that cannot be bought or paid for,
and cannot be replaced.**

Do be patient with people, you never know what the next
man or woman is going through or has been through
to become them.

**Learn to tell yourself you can do,
learn to be positive and self-encouraging.**

Don't be so hard on yourself, you've been through a lot.

**Mistakes are a natural part of growth, and many times
before great success comes great failures.**

It takes much more energy to hold hate for something
than to love, harbor not hatred or negative feelings
towards others.

**Learn to let the small mistakes fade away as the greater
things in love develop.**

In everyday is the opportunity to be a better you,
or to try to make better choices in life.

**Sometimes you have to go right
when everyone wants you to go left.**

When you get to where you're going,
you'll find God right there waiting for you.

**Sometimes we have to set aside our ego's
and pick up our hearts.**

If you are happy and satisfied with where you are in life,
and you know what you are doing is good,
you are successful.

Desire not the attention, acceptance or praise of others, but accept oneself and know you are a work in progress.

If you're doing your best at something, be satisfied with your current progress as you move forward through growth, know inside yourself you are giving your all.

It is a gift to be.

Criticize not the efforts of others, compare not persons as this is apples to oranges.

Many times, the harder we try at something the harder it gets, but remember resistance builds strength.

To make something better you don't amplify or multiply that which is wrong, you reinforce and multiply its positive.

I believe in people and I believe in their positive potentials.

Avoid impulsiveness as it is fools rush in.

A calm, clear, focused mind will find more answers than a stressed, cluttered one will.

Before I write I usually take a moment to settle my thoughts and clear my mind of the day's stresses, worries or anxieties.

Sometimes it helps to forget where you are to find yourself.

Humble men make good friends.

You're not alone, it is together we are.

Some days I laugh and smile, and some days I cry. Yet it is every day I am grateful for.

What doesn't break a man, can make a man.
I believe we cannot be broken, only fortified as people.

**When I doubt myself or my capabilities as a person,
I remind myself He believes in me.**

I think the most important thing you should know,
is that yes, you are loved.

**When I felt as if I had nothing to give you,
I gave you my thoughts. I gave you me.**

Act not in haste, but with love and patience.

Even on a rainy day I can find a reason to smile.

You can hate me because I gave you love,
and that says what?

**It's not me or my work I need you to recognize,
it's your own positive potentials.**

When Angels and demons collide,
nothing is left but God's love.

**A broke man with wisdom will forever
be richer than a wealthy fool.**

You can sell your soul for riches,
but you cannot sell your riches for soul.

**If success in this world was based on goodness of heart,
I'd win. Since it is based on your value of material things
I lose here.**

To you I may be losing, I'm not rich.
To you I may be a failure,
I have no social status or accolades.
Yet it is in God's eyes I'm a champion.

**My real dream inside was to help you,
and to optimize your positive potential
as well as the overall experience of life on earth.**

I've been beaten but never broken,
I've been knocked down but never out.
You can't defeat a man who refuses to give up.

**Sometimes you have to lose many times
before you see victory.**

Your love will forever be stronger than their hate.

**No obstacle you will encounter
is in all ways greater than you.**

You can't break me, God made me.

If God's all you got, you'll in all ways have all you need.

It's not a question of how, or why. It just is,
and I appreciate that.

**You deserve to smile, you deserve to laugh.
You deserve better days.**
I'll invest my time to help give you what God gave you.

Humanity is beautiful.

**We should always take a moment to give thanks to those
who pave the paths on which we tread,
it wasn't always this easy or possible.**

We should always remember and give time and moments
of remembrance to those who have come before us.
Spend a moment appreciating.

**Look around you, spend a moment being grateful.
Look what you have been given, even if you have paid for
those things someone thought to create it for you.**

Hey, have a beautiful day.

**When you get to where you're going,
you'll find God right there waiting for you.**

HE paid a price I couldn't afford, so it is to HIM,
and to you I dedicate my time.

**Do be loyal to your friends,
do be understanding and fast to forgive.**

We are not perfect, people make mistakes.
Yet these mistakes need not be fatal, do be forgiving.

**Embrace one another as friends and family, encourage
the gathering of peoples to praise God and share his word.**

None, not one of our problems are bigger than our God
or his love for us.

HE died for my sins, so I choose to live for HIS love.

When they throw dirt on your name,
when they curse you pray for them.
Prayer is powerful and the Lord is with you.

**The Lord's love be with you wherever it is you may go,
carry with you HIS love and in this way share this love.**

Pray for your enemies, pray for love to be with them and
watch as the Lord converts your enemies to friends.

Never give up on you, HE doesn't.

Whatever you're going through, trust in the Lord
and you'll get through it with HIM.
It is with God all things are possible.

I lean not on my own understandings,
but on that the God's plan for me is greater than mine.

Focus or center your attention on the good things,
on that which is and not on that which is not.

**Learn to tell yourself you can do it, you are beautiful
and you can do all things through Christ
who strengthens you.**

Rest your worries,
rest your anxieties and lean on your faith.

**It might not be okay all the time,
but with Him you'll be alright.**

When we come together in His name,
there's not an evil in existence that can stop that love.

**It takes much courage to walk a straight path through
a crooked world, yet it is with God all things are possible.**

If you seek Him with all your heart,
it is Him you will find.

**Confess to Him your fears
and it is courage you be blessed with.**

He knows you, and He also knows how to straighten
paths which have been made crooked.
He knows how to comfort you.

**There is no doubt in my mind,
without the love of the Lord I would be not here today.**

I'm blessed, and it is to and for Him I am grateful.

**It is my joy to spread love and to be in doing so
an extension of His reach.**

It is easier to help, than to hurt. It is easier to love than to hate. It is when you give you truly receive.

**As is true the Lord gave sight to the blind,
His love can illuminate the darkest of hearts.**

Invest in the hearts and minds of all,
you will find yourself greatly rewarded.

**Carry with you His love wherever it is you may go,
so that it is there it too be as well.**

Arm yourselves with the word of God,
as it can serve as both sword and shield.

**When you love the Lord with all your heart,
and accept Him as your savior you receive His blessings
and favor. Beautiful things begin to happen in your life.**

If love is your anchor and the Lord is your savior, not
even a sea of hatred could move you or alter your way.

**Do embrace one another as friends and family,
enjoy each other's company and companionship.**

Appreciate the character and individuality of others.
You are you and I am I, and that's a beautiful thing.

**Like a good breakfast, the word of God in our minds
and the Lord's love in our hearts helps us to prepare
to face the world.**

When someone cares for you, they'll speak good of your
name, if they don't, they'll gossip behind your back.

Avoid having two faces,
show everyone the same love and respect.

When you accept the fact that at times
life is challenging, it gives you the chance
to turn those challenges into opportunities.

Do be very slow to anger and very fast to forgive.
An angry fool's never a wise man.

The Lord is my strength, He is my salvation.
He delivers me from evil
and provides me shelter from the storm.

When your faith in Him, is greater than the hatred
or negativity of the worlds you can conquer any task
at hand.

Always believe in Him, as He loves you
and will be with you wherever it is you may go.
Through good times and through bad.

When I felt like no one would be there for me
or understand me, He was and did because
He loves me as He too loves you.

When you truly believe, when you truly have faith in Him
the impossible is possible as He knows.
All ways trust God.

**If you would like to make the devil nervous,
love thy neighbor as thyself. Embrace one another
as friends and family.**

Satan works diligently and knows very well his time
is limited. Love will conquer hatred. Let him not
steal your joy or taint your days.

**I hope you have a very beautiful love filled day.
God bless you.**

Wise is to give glory to God,
and to be not prideful in our ways.

**There's something very beautiful about believing
and having faith in Jesus, in that without Him we are
partial and it is our firm faith that completes us.**

Sometimes we all fall, yet it's not the fall that matters
it's that you get back up with the courage to try again.

**When you live by, and obey the word of God,
miraculous things begin to happen in your favor and
impossible is nothing.**

Trust in Him with all your heart, lean on Him
in times of need and you can make it through anything.
It is with Him all things are possible.

**With faith in the Lord, and love as your compass
you can navigate even the toughest of times.**

When I feel empty or alone, I'm reminded His love
is all I need and that He be with me wherever I go
and I'm then refreshed and renewed.

**To Him I am forever grateful, it is by way of His love
I am whole, and in this sense complete
and in process of progress.**

We're all works in progress, we are beautiful and in our
own ways unique yet it is as God's children we are one.

**Be not afraid to make mistakes, as human beings it is
and will be a natural part of our growth process.**

As it is everything I have been given begins as a gift
from God, and secondly friends and family,
to Him I am forever grateful and wish not to take
but to give, and to receive His blessing in doing so.

**To give is to receive and it be my joy to do so.
My true heart of hearts and honest intent is simply to
help and to assist that which God has created with no
ulterior motive or expectation.**

I enjoy seeing you do well and I enjoy seeing you smile.
I wish you a very beautiful prosperous existence.

**If you wish to be close to God, allow the light of love
to guide you there. You are of love I remind you,
and God is love.**

It is of great importance to invite the Lord into your life
as it is with Him all things are possible.
Allow Him to help and assist you.

**The most important decision we can make in our lives
is to give our lives to God, in doing so we become
whole beings of His love.**

The Lord is my shepherd, righteousness is of me said He and ways of the wicked shall perish but he who do the will of God shall live forever.

Do love one another as friends and as family, as this is the way.

God loves us, He who created all who created is for us and not against us.

When we let go of our wants, and keep our would likes, we allow God to work miracles in our lives and receive His blessings.

It seems as if life's not a question of who can love through love. It's who can love through hate? because that's a real challenge we face.

As a child I told myself the stars could hear my wishes, I still believe this to be true.

Choose to see the good in people, choose to forgive their mistakes as we are all works in progress.

Even a good man is capable of doing bad or wrong.

Value the kindness others choose to show you,
as these are choices people have made in your favor.

**If you don't forgive other's mistakes,
how can you expect them to forgive yours?**

I am a champion of the Lord's, and am this because
I believe in Him and I believe it is He who saved me.

**Practice acceptance. Be patient with yourself
and accept that you too are a work in progress.**

God made us very able. God made us so we can do,
we can accomplish and do all things through Christ
who strengthens us.

**Practice positive thinking actively,
do develop positive tendency.**

Do be considerate of others, be aware of one another
and respect each other as individuals.

Sometimes a little consideration can go a long way.

A heightened sense of awareness and increased
concentration of observation accelerates the elevation
of consideration you feel.

**It is much easier to lift a person up than to push one
down. Everyone would like to be uplifted at times and
none wish to be pushed down.**

Never hold on when you need to let go,
never let go when you need to hold on.

**To succeed in this life, one must be willing to risk
the humiliation of failure, and have the courage
to continue pursuit after such.**

You can choose to count a man's failures,
or you can choose to count what counts: that he tried.

When you speak badly upon the names of others,
it speaks volumes about yourself.

You cannot fortify falsities against truths in a permanent manner as it is truth is fully fortified in original form and it need not lies to exist.

Behind every lie is a reason, and behind every smile isn't always the truth.

It takes courage to stand and sit at the same time. Remember that.

Often times during debates we find one side backed by truthful factual information and the other by falsified opinionated observations.

In most cases upon exposing, examining, and inspecting information close observation of details will lead to discrepancies in such if such is false.

There's at least two sides to every story, and one's usually right.

Behind every good man is a good woman.

Are you happy in your present state, if not practice the identifying of the reasons why.

For one to achieve one must first sight specific goals or target objectives.

To conquer your days and seize success in the opportunities presented one must properly prioritize.

**A little consideration goes a long way.
It is together we are I remind you.**

Learn to let go of anything mentally holding you back, focus on positive progress.

**Did you know you could be someone's turning point?
You can be someone's game changer
and alter the course of their life for the better.**

One smile can change the world, as every smile does.

Almost any lasting success takes practice, persistence, and perseverance to achieve.

It helps to break large goals down into a series of mini-goals to accomplish. Doing that will help you achieve the big goal.

It was known, it was written.

You can ask a man to go a certain way,
but until he learns for himself and is convinced
that's the right way he'll go his own way.

My heart is yours. Here it is, take it you can have it.

I go through it and you go through it.
Yet we go through it together.

You are not alone.

We are people, we are human beings.
It doesn't matter your color, or your race.
Love is love, and that's a universal language.

In or during stressful times I find it best to lean on my faith and trust in God's timing.

A pencil is a beautiful thing, combined with the imagination or creativity of a human being and possibilities are endless.

Good, positive, healthy, happy fun time is essential. Everyone needs to have some fun, some times.

When going through a lot of mental stress, it's important to maintain or find a healthy balance.

Sometimes all we have to do is wait it out, and sometimes all we have to do is act now.

If something is positive or non-destructive to either itself or the whole, and is in its natural state best is to leave it be unless innovation or alteration of one or more aspects of such will provide improvement in some way or another.

We're all works in progress.

Life is a story of all for all,
everyone gets a chapter in this book.

**Engineer your dreams, design your destination.
Live, breathe and be, it is with God all things are possible.**

If someone said you couldn't, you may just believe them,
always have faith in you and know that again,
it is with God all things are possible.

**There is no limit to your imagination or
capabilities in time.**

You are loved.

**Do develop can-do mentalities,
it is where there is a will there will always be a way.**

Let or permit or allow the love in your hearts to serve
as your guiding light.

Without you I would be lonely.

Be easy. Be fast to forgive and slow to anger.

Always believe in you, God does.

If you choose to take what you have learned
and you choose to carry that with you,
even bad days can become good ones.

A moment of understanding can last a lifetime.

Never give up on love.

Love will never give up on you.

A loss isn't a loss if a lesson's learned.

Everything you've been through made you who you are.

Sometimes our losses teach us more than our victories.

**You cannot be broken,
only strengthened so as to be fortified.**

Sometimes what we want for, or in our lives is not
what God knows we need for, or in our lives.

**Change is a natural part of our existence,
accept those challenges.**

As a rivers waters erode the banks
and carve its way through the lands,
the trials and tribulations we go through create
lasting impressions on the souls of each man.

**Ever notice that every dreamer believed that he could?
And the words of the doubters fell upon deaf ears,
so to speak.**

Sometimes we have to blind ourselves to the negativity,
sometimes we have to choose to hear the hope and believe
in ourselves as well as our dreams.

**My dream was to help you achieve yours,
and in these books, I see myself doing so.**

Your value is of infinite measure,
for you the possibilities are limitless.

**Do you know the possibilities of a life?
Just look at what God so chose to do with His.**

I do as I do, because I believe in Him
and that which He has created.

Today is a beautiful day.
Though I may see struggles in and through such
tomorrow will see a better version of me.

There is no doubt in my mind or in my heart that I would
not be who I am or be this strong without the love of God.
Without the love of His Son,
I would be not who I am today.

Easy is to forgive one's friends,
difficult is to forgive one's enemies.

If one could blur the lines of our indifference's,
and set aside that which separates us we would see unity
in a whole new light and love in new ways.

If one wishes to see change, one must become change.

The heart of a child is but the softest thing,
I pray a rugged world hardens it not.

We should celebrate each other's existence,
and in doing so share that appreciation
of one another with one another.

God does not utilize new life to subtract from that which is, you are a positive addition to life and all that is.

Do embrace you, express yourself and share your story.

Life is a love story.

**It is prideful ways that separates us,
and understanding and compassion that makes us whole.**

Sometimes we place ourselves on pedestals higher than others, in such case humility is sometimes necessary to humble oneself.

Underneath our egos is an underlying need to be noticed, loved and appreciated. When we strip away that and realize we are all loved we all become the stars we are.

Every breath, every touch, every sight I've seen was a gift to me. For this I am forever grateful and it is to Him I dedicate my time.

If the choice was yours to either score the game winning points or provide the assist, which would you choose?

Never give up on you, God doesn't.

In argumentative conversations there is a proper way to contradict each other's intelligence or knowledge without belittling.

When contradicting someone best is to base such on facts and technicalities currently at hand rather than personal preference or opinion.

If I could I'd battle every demon in existence so you would have to battle none.

Time is precious. Choose wisely what you invest yours in.

In a blank page I see infinite possibility.

To be inspired is one of the greatest gifts one can be given. The aftermath of such can be remarkably exceptionally beautiful.

It's not always the results that matter so much as the process by which one achieves such. Meaning sometimes the journey is more important than the destination.

In everything is a lesson to be learned.

Take your time and pace yourself as patience is a virtue.

Take it easy on you, you are a beautiful work of art in process of progress.

Feed your brain positivity and disregard negative thoughts as just that.

Balance your time and try not to always work.
Balance is essential to a healthy life.

**We have no idea what each other has been through
or is still going through daily, judge not.**

With a page and a pen,
a man or woman can change the world forevermore.

Be caring, be considerate, be compassionate.

Humble men make great friends.
Gentle souls make good guys.

You are not alone.

I gave you me.

**If one of my writings affects one person in a positive way,
I feel I have succeeded.**

Each and every one of us is meant to be,
God doesn't make mistakes.

A smile can change the world forever.

Engage not in petty quarrels,
make not mountains of mole hills.

Be kind.

If I wasn't this way this wouldn't be this way.

**Some people need to be catered to so to speak
while others need to do the catering.**

If you are privileged and or fortunate,
good is to give back.

**What we do comes back to us,
yet only God knows when and how.**

God knew before He made the earth that
I would be right here in this very chair
at this very moment writing this very book.

**To the Father, to the Son, and to the Holy Spirit
I'm forever grateful.**

There is a huge difference between that which is mentally
thought, that which is verbally spoken, and that which
is physically done. Do be positive.

**Choose to never be defeated. Take what you have learned
from a situation and apply it elsewhere in your life.**

Life is beautiful, beautiful is life.

I do not believe that people as entire beings can be broken, I believe our handicaps strengthen us elsewhere and that our struggles enhance our character.

Let the Lord guide you, allow yourself
to be the love you are.

Listen to your heart.

You were not born to fit in, you were born to stand out.

The Lord is my savior, it is with Him that I am whole.

When you release your expectation of worldly things, you receive Godly blessings.

To the Lord I say, "I know not where You are, yet I know You are, and it is to You I am forever grateful."

We are not alone.

To be me was a fight fought. To deliver to you these words I gave my life, I invested my time.

I work diligently because I know the enemy will stop at nothing to see me defeated.

You can walk this mile, but not in these shoes.

Not wise is to criticize others, in doing so one speaks volumes of oneself.

Knowing I cannot better anything less than my best, I always try to try.

The first step to achieving is believing.

Yes, you can. It is with God all things are possible.

Sometimes all we need is a few positive words of encouragement.

**Visualize the path to your goals,
plan ahead and pave that road.**

Keep your thoughts positive,
your heart pure and your intentions good as you proceed.

Have you told anyone you love them today?

I promised myself I'd never give up,
and that I would never lose hope.

**When you detach yourself from the results of your work
and focus on the work itself you in all actuality reap
greater rewards.**

We all wish to be recognized for our achievements
or efforts and noticed so to speak for such, yet do know
this: God knows. Though on earth you may struggle,
in Heaven you will be blessed for serving Him.

**I dream of a day our doors are unlocked,
and our children play safely amongst one another
while parents rest their worries.**

I believe that, if you dive into a sea of what is thought
to be hatred for love, love will see you through.

**Though the majority of my time is spent alone
I know that I am not.**

I spend many nights pondering, many days thinking,
many hours and minutes investing my heart into helping
and assisting that which God has created
because I believe in Him, and you.

**Because He is my savior, because He is my salvation
I carry the cross.**

His love is unflawed, He is perfect in all His ways.

Most certainly because it is here now it once was not,
yet it is because of His love that it be.

Love is a language every heart speaks fluently.

Always be grateful. Life is a gift.

There is something to learn from everyone.

**Each one, every person brings something
very special into existence.**

You have limitless potential, and unlimited possibilities.
You can be, and you can do anything your heart desires.
With God all things are possible.

Internal peace, external peace.

Your happiness, hold that.

Your extraordinarily magnificent.
You are incredibly strong.
You were created by God.
You cannot be broken, only fortified.

Learn to see life for what it is, appreciate what you have, and not focus on what it's not or which may be missing. We are, and have been, truly blessed.

God is good.

Live now.

Every day is amazing, every day is beautiful.

In this book, within these pages I choose to bare my soul.

It is of love you are I remind you.

Within my heart rests a message, and I believe this
message to be from God: You, are loved.

To step forward and proceed with love is to act in belief.

Do be optimistic, keep a positive perspective on all things.

You can do anything you tell yourself you can do.

Though at times my life is quite the struggle,
it is with honor I serve Him and a pleasure to do so.

**Release your expectations of the days
and each will become a blessing.**

Give more, expect less.

Trust God.

This book is dedicated to You.

As well as to my daughter:

Aaliyah Alt

God Bless your hearts.

You, Are Love.

www.ingramcontent.com/pod-product-compliance
Lightning Source LLC
LaVergne TN
LVHW021825060526
838201LV00058B/3514